GW01392973

Project Art Works

Art in Transition

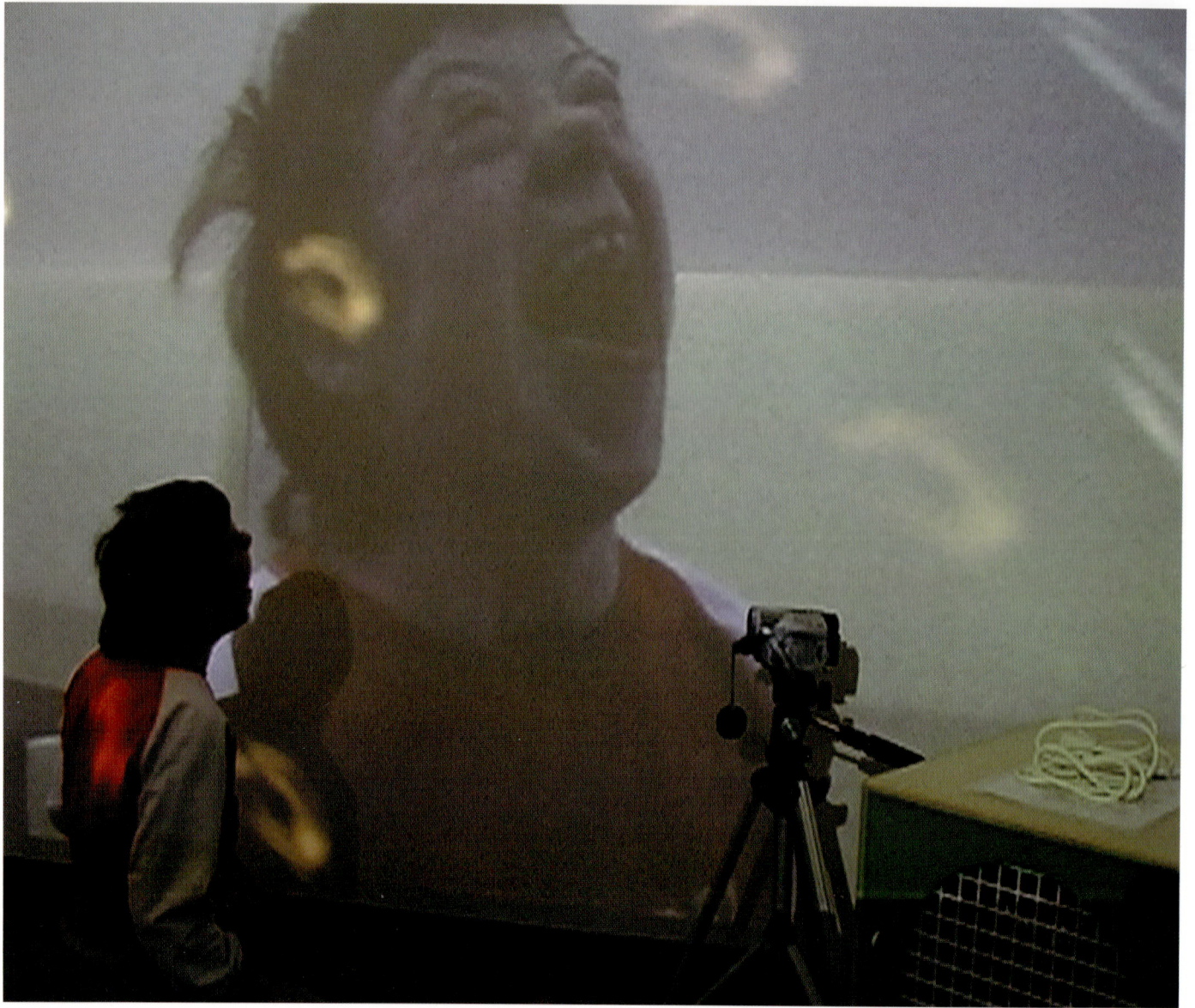

Project Art Works

Art in Transition

**The Personal Profile Project
2005–2008**
A creative intervention in the
transition of young people
with complex needs from
children's to adult services

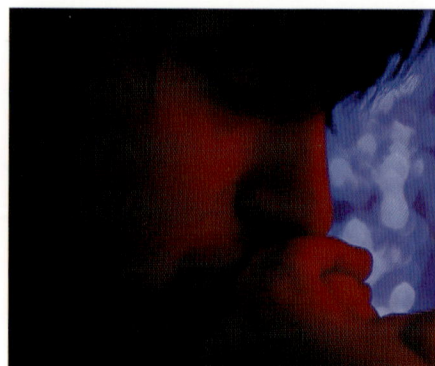

Contents

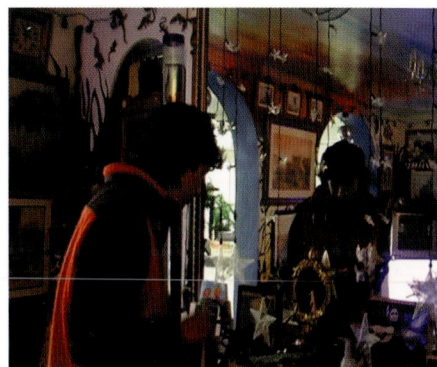

Foreword

Between 2000 and 2002, my family and I experienced the process of supporting our son Paul, who has complex needs, through the formal transition from school to adult life. This is a time of hope and anxiety for most parents. For the family of a young man who is unable to articulate his needs, desires and opinions *verbally* but who is vital, aware and enthusiastic about all aspects of his life, the shared navigation of this transition was fraught with uncertainty.

The process involved a lot of thinking and reflection on what might constitute a well structured and flexible support plan for Paul and the family as a whole. We wanted him to continue enjoying his life and be supported in exploring his potential, whilst staying safe and well cared for, but our plans were, and remain, subject to local authority funding decisions and the continuing uncertainty of changes in policy and political climates.

The formal process involved Paul and his family in assessments and meetings with multiple agencies, teachers and his social worker. The information was collated into a formal Assessment of Need, which would be used to inform funding decisions about future provision. The assessment was detailed but focused almost exclusively on the extent and nature of Paul's disabilities and care needs. There was very little information about who he is and how he engages with, and perceives, the world. Many of these facets of his personality and individuality are enigmatic and subtle but a good understanding of them is vital to his wellbeing.

As an artist and co-founder of Project Art Works, an arts organisation that specialises in working with young people with complex needs, I began to think hard about the experience of transition and how we as an organisation might harness some of the approaches we have used in other situations, to use art to reveal the individuality of young people with severe neurological impairments.

Good artists are observant. They are accustomed to visually scrutinising and translating the world. At Project Art Works we work with artists who are exceptionally skilled at using different art media to connect with people who use few or none of the formal, learnt methods of interaction. In our experience, film can be used as a multi-sensory tool capable of communicating subtle facts, ideas and information without the necessity of verbal description.

The film-based Personal Profile Project was designed to provide a creative framework in which artists would collaborate with12 individual young people and produce a short film with each of them that would illuminate the subtle and inconspicuous signifiers in the way they communicate and express themselves, as well as showing them going about their daily lives. The films would, we hoped, add another dimension to the formal assessments of need and enhance the transition process for everyone involved.

We are extremely grateful to the 12 young people who took part, to their families, friends, teachers, social workers and support workers and all the artists involved who so fully embraced the collaborative ethos of the project. We hope you find the story of the project contained in these pages interesting and illuminating.

Kate Adams
Director, Project Art Works

Project Art Works is a visual arts organisation that works with children and adults with complex needs. A person with complex needs has at least two types of severe or profound disability and needs intensive and specialised support to fulfil his or her potential and to get the most out of life.

The Personal Profile Project grew out of Project Art Works' extensive experience of making art with young people in school and community settings and its interest in developing the role that film might play in easing the transition every young person with complex needs must make from school to adult life.

Young people with severe intellectual disability can experience profound exclusion from society. This is the result of a number of factors including:

- the necessity for highly skilled support in physical, communication and personal care needs;
- lack of accessible public/private environments;
- other people's response to severe disability;
- intensive behavioural management support to enable community integration;
- the limitations of the services and provision that young people depend upon;
- family stress and isolation.

Project Art Works recognises that meaningful integration for young people who have severe intellectual disabilities takes time, understanding, insight and resources. This pilot project enabled young people's voices to be heard and to have a role in decision making through artist films that explored, reflected and made visible their particular and individual qualities, preferences and ways of communicating.

Transition planning

In England, when young people with a statement of special educational needs are preparing to leave school, they go through a process known as transition planning. This involves teachers, social workers and health care professionals, such as speech therapists and physiotherapists, working with the young person, their family members and support workers to assess their needs and interests and to identify opportunities for them, once they leave school.

This can be a stressful time for young people and for their families, who may feel uncertain about what the future holds. This is especially so for a young person with *severe* learning disabilities who needs a great deal of support, all day, every day, in order to live life as fully as possible. Leaving school means a significant adjustment to new people, new environments, new activities and routines and all this needs to be taken into account by the transition planning process. Questions that need to be asked include:

- What are the young person's hopes and aspirations for the future and how can these be met?
- Will parents experience new care needs and require practical help?
- How can young people be enabled to have a role in their community?
- Does the young person have any special health or welfare needs that will require planning and support from health and social services now or in the future?
- Will funding be awarded to enable the 'plan' to become a reality?

The challenge for many young people is how to be meaningfully involved in the processes of identifying and describing their own desires and needs for the future; how to be understood by the new services and people in their lives. Ideally, every individual should have the opportunity to express his or her preferences, likes and dislikes and hopes. If, however, he or she finds it difficult to understand, or does not communicate with words or language, the transition process has to rely on paper-based descriptions and assessments to convey often subtle and complex information.

Despite the gradual introduction of person-centred approaches to reviews and transition planning, many young people who have complex support needs are still defined and described through headings and systems designed and implemented by others. Social care services still struggle with the complexities of meaningful consultation with these groups of young people.

It was against this background that Project Art Works set about designing the Personal Profile Project, to test the impact of creative interventions in the transition planning process of 12 young people in South East England.

In 2004, it invited the Camelot Foundation to get involved and to the Foundation's lasting credit, it agreed to fund a two-year pilot project. Arts Council England South East and East Sussex Learning Disability Development Fund also made significant financial contributions.

When the Personal Profile Project was conceived, many of the young people with whom Project Art Works had been working for some years were approaching the end of their time at school. In some cases, the visual arts (painting, drawing, three-dimensional installations, photography and film) had played an important part in their educational and personal development. The Project Art Works team was concerned that the transition planning process might not pick up on the level of creativity and enthusiasm for art they had experienced and they began to think about other ways in which the interests and abilities of a young person with complex needs might be communicated.

Project Art Works proposed that a short film, made by an artist, in collaboration with a young person and showing him or her in a variety of social, environmental and creative contexts, with and without family, teachers and friends, could positively inform the transition process. It would complement the other forms of documentation and assessment and illuminate the discussion between parents and professionals about the young person's interests, abilities, attributes and needs.

The project had seven aims. These were to:
- help young people with profound and complex disabilities to communicate something about how they perceive the world;
- facilitate a better understanding of each young person (beyond their disability) by describing their preferences and individual qualities, in ways that would be accessible and poetic;
- help young people and their families to feel better understood and more in control of the choices they make;
- complement the transition process that the young people and families were going through;
- facilitate greater participation in the assessment and description of a young person through art;
- produce a self-determined and expressive body of art-based information;
- determine whether a package could be created to inspire other transition services across the country.

The national picture

The Personal Profile Project coincided with a period of reflection, research and policy development in relation to adult social care, on the part of government, the voluntary sector and grant-making trusts. In 1998, the Department of Health had launched its *Modernisation of Adult Social Care* initiative and in 2003, it had commissioned a series of research projects to evaluate the impact of the initiative, five years on. The findings of these research projects were published in *Modernising Adult Social Care – what's working*, in June 2007. Also, in January that year, the Commission for Social Care Inspection had published *Growing Up Matters*, its report on better transition planning for young people with complex needs.

The aims and the timing of the pilot of the Personal Profile Project were right and the funding was in place. Now it was up to Project Art Works to translate those aims into action, to record what happened and to share the lessons learned with other young people, their families and the professionals involved in transition planning elsewhere in the country.

Who took part

The project was organised in two phases. The first phase, which ran from spring 2005 to summer 2006, involved eight young people and four artists. The second phase, which ran from autumn 2006 to summer 2007, involved four young people and four artists, two of whom also worked on phase one.

The first group of young people were pupils at Hazel Court School in Eastbourne and Glyne Gap School in Bexhill on Sea. Seven of the eight places were taken by young people with complex needs and the eighth went to a young woman with much less severe learning difficulties. The second group were pupils at Downs View College in Brighton and Ickburgh School in the London Borough of Hackney.

Below is a list of the young people who took part and the name of the artist with whom they made their film.

	Young person	Artist
Phase 1	Beteena Apps	Annis Joslin
	Liam Ash	Tim Corrigan
	Sophie Bristow	Shona Illingworth
	Hannah Cottingham	Shona Illingworth
	Claire Day	Tim Corrigan
	Mark Fraser	Andrew Kötting
	Loren Jerome	Annis Joslin
	Cherry Lane	Andrew Kötting
Phase 2	Anisa Mayet	Charlotte Ginsborg
	Helen Snowden	Annis Joslin
	Jack Stephenson	Ben Rivers
	Husne Tekagac	Tim Corrigan and Charlotte Ginsborg

Although some of the young people had worked with Project Art Works before and most had some experience of working with photography and video, no one had been involved in a film-making project before.

The artists who made the films use film or video as all or part of their artistic practice. For this project they were presented with the challenge of working with a young person, to produce a film of high quality, lasting between ten and fifteen minutes; a film that would be accessible and poetic; a film that would help others to know its subject better.

Some artists accumulated several hours of footage, leaving the camera running throughout their meetings with the young people. Others stopped filming once they had captured a scene. In most cases, the artist showed some of their rough work to the young person and where possible, asked for feedback. Rough versions of the final films were shared with the other artists, the director of Project Art Works and the project coordinator before the final version was produced.

The participation of family members, friends, support workers, teachers and others varied from person to person. In some cases, this wider circle of contacts played a significant role in the film-making process and featured in the final film. In other cases, they had relatively little involvement.

Triangle, a Brighton-based organisation that specialises in consulting people with learning disabilities was asked, by Project Art Works, to watch the final films with the young people and their families and to ask for their consent to show the work more widely. The following pages present words and images from each of the films.

Young person
Cherry Lane

Artist
Andrew Kötting

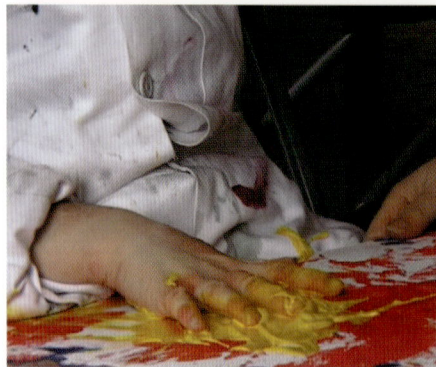

"I THINK SHE'D LIKE NOT TO BE UNDERESTIMATED AND TO CONTINUE TO AMAZE PEOPLE BY WHAT SHE CAN DO AS OPPOSED TO WHAT SHE CAN'T. I THINK THAT SHE WOULD VERY MUCH LIKE A CAREER TRAINING ARTISTS TO WORK WITH PEOPLE LIKE HER. SHE'S VERY CUT OUT FOR THAT." (CHERRY'S MOTHER)

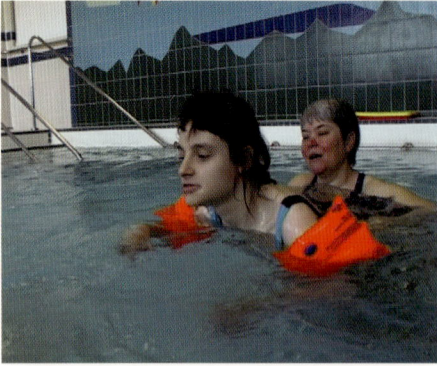
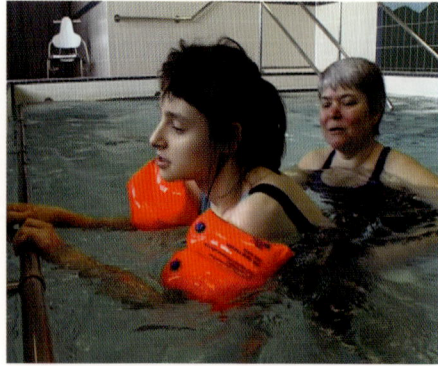
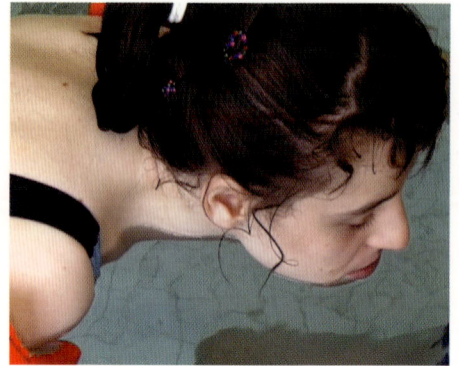

"WHEN SHE'S OKAY AND SHE'S FAIRLY OPTIMISTIC ABOUT THE PEOPLE AROUND HER UNDERSTANDING, SHE HAS A WHOLE RANGE OF PERSONALITIES – DEVIOUS AND CHEEKY RIGHT THROUGH TO DEEPLY CARING." (CHERRY'S MOTHER)

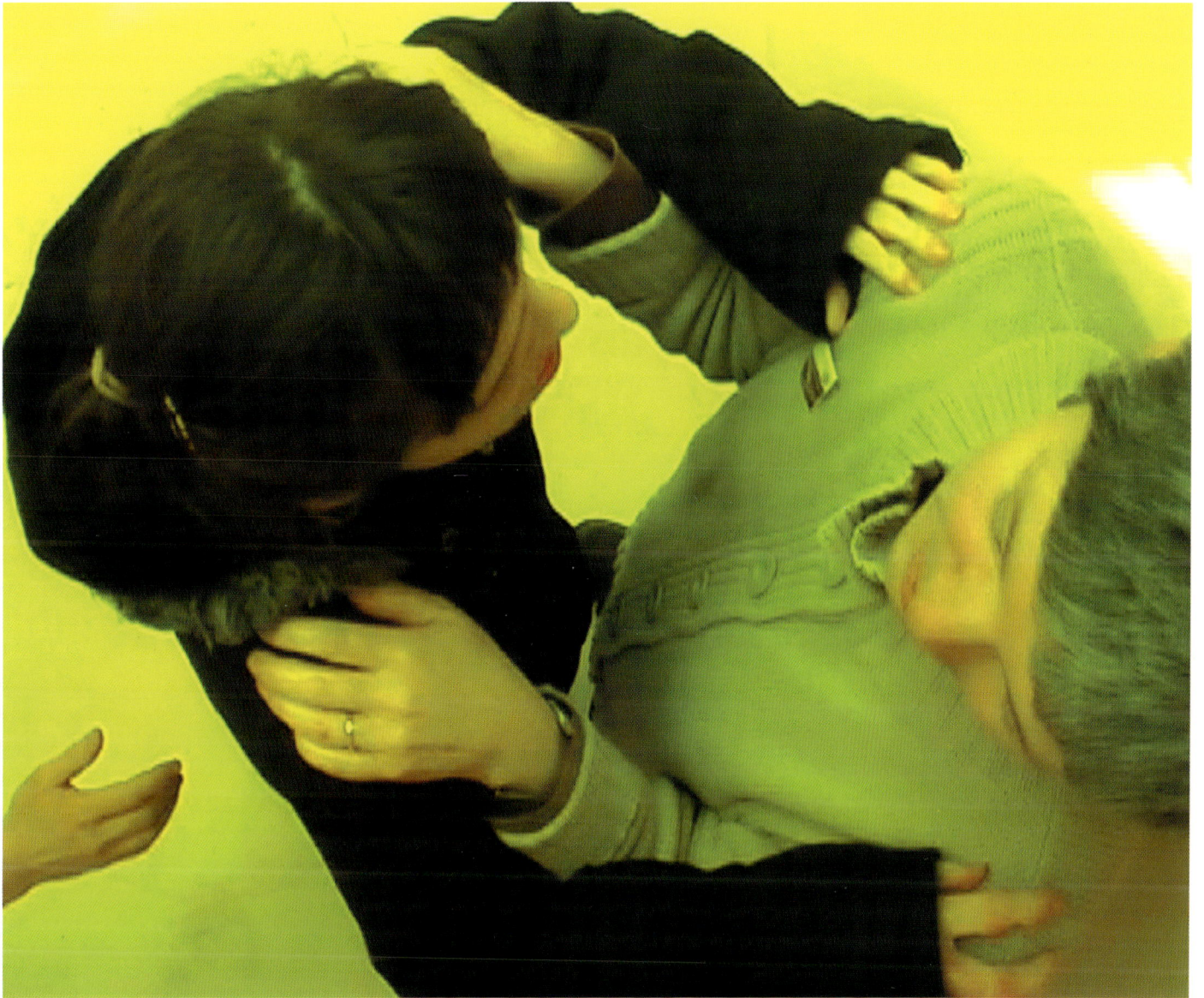

"ALL THROUGH HER SCHOOL LIFE, COMMUNICATION HAS BEEN THE THING THAT WE'VE WORKED HARDEST ON, TO GIVE CHERRY THE TOOLS TO COMMUNICATE... WE REALISED IT WASN'T JUST UP TO HER TO COMMUNICATE WITH US, BUT IT WAS UP TO US TO BEGIN TO LEARN HER LANGUAGE." (CHERRY'S MOTHER)

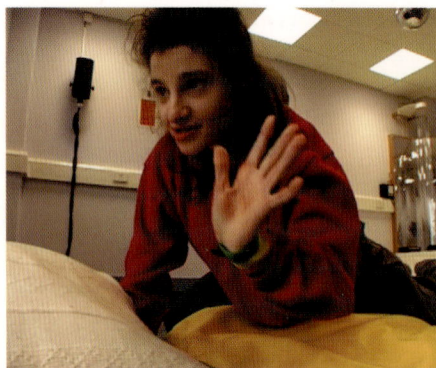

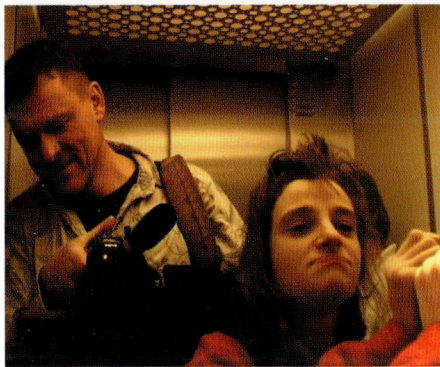

MARK ENJOYS BEING WITH HIS FRIENDS.

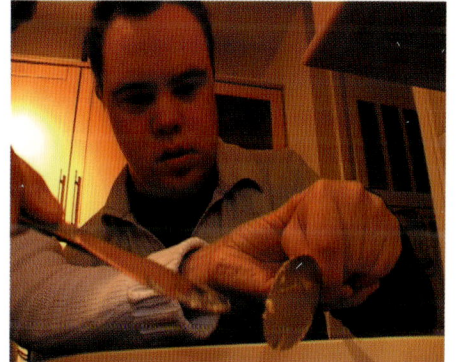

HE LIKES MAKING CAKES, WHILE LISTENING TO MUSIC.

pizza

chips

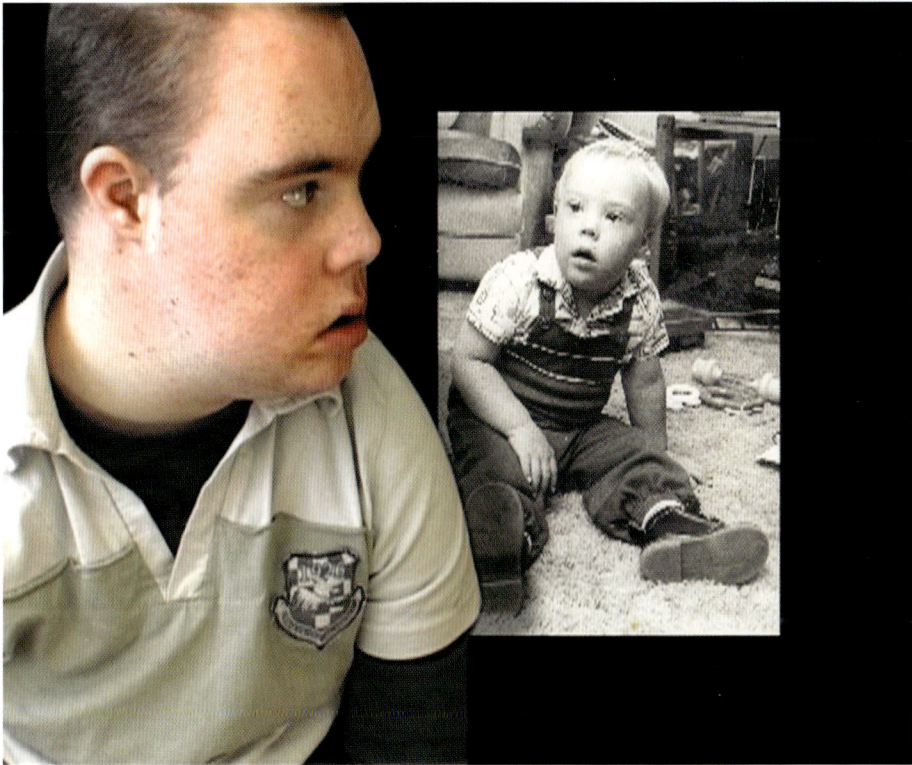

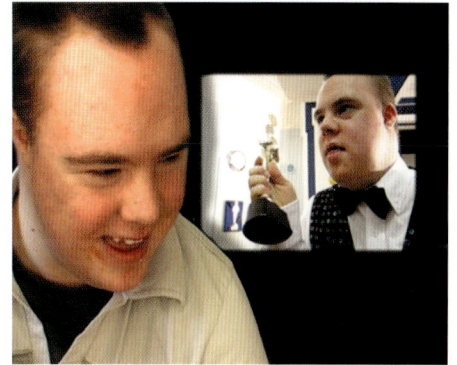

HE ENJOYS WORKING IN THE GARDEN
RUN BY THE PARCHMENT TRUST.

Mark Fraser | Andrew Kötting

Young person
Anisa Mayet

Artist
Charlotte Ginsborg

"I CAN'T WAIT TO GO BACK TO SCHOOL. I MISS MY FRIENDS."

"IN A NEW SITUATION SHE CAN LACK CONFIDENCE BUT BEING WITH SOME FRIENDS WILL HELP HER." (ANISA'S TEACHER)

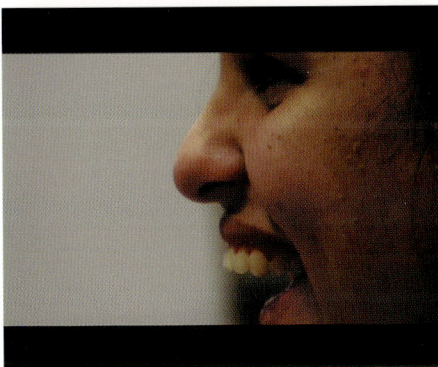

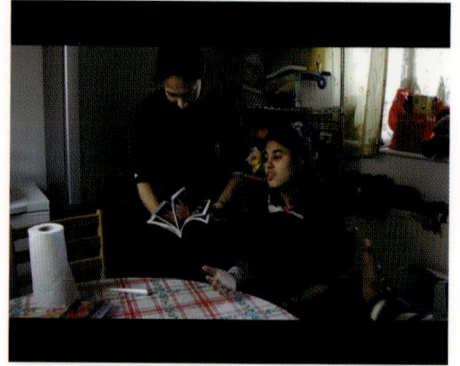

"SHE DOES ON THE WHOLE HAVE A GOOD ABILITY TO COMMUNICATE AND GETS HER MESSAGE ACROSS QUITE WELL AND HAS A FANTASTIC SENSE OF HUMOUR. SHE CAN TALK THE HIND LEGS OFF A DONKEY." (ANISA'S TEACHER)

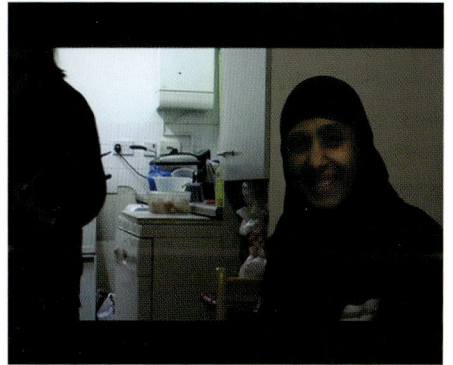

"WHERE WOULD YOU DRIVE IN YOUR CAR ANISA?"
"INDIA!"

"SHE LOVES SONGS. SHE LIKES SHOPPING." (ANISA'S MOTHER)
"AND P.E.!"

Young person
Claire Day

Artist
Tim Corrigan

"WE'RE BIGGER THAN HER, BUT SHE'S OLDER."
(CLAIRE'S FRIEND)

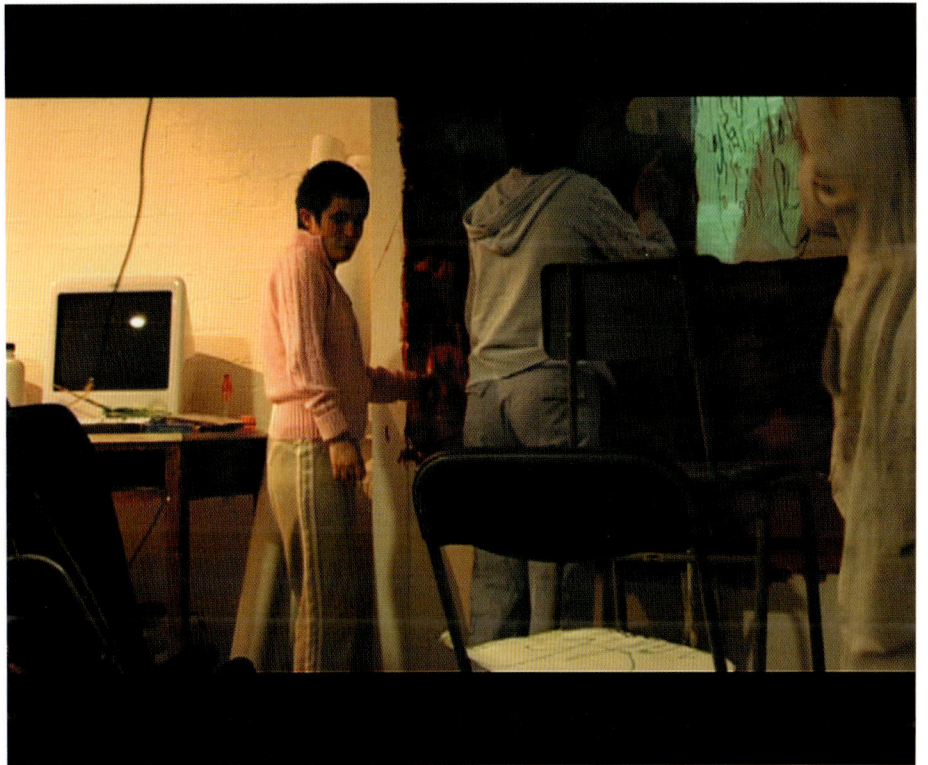

"SHE'S KIND, SHY, QUIET."
(CLAIRE'S FRIEND)

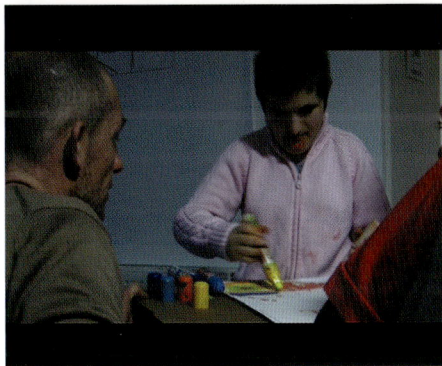

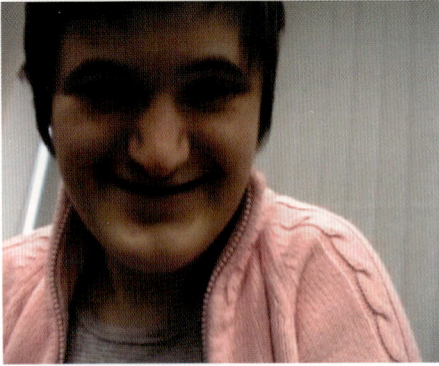

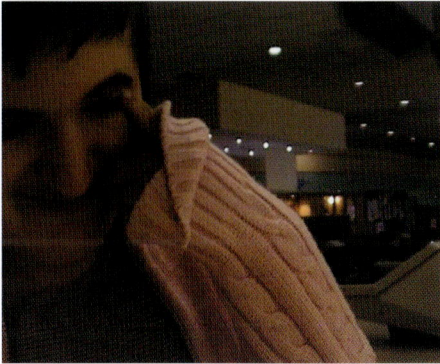

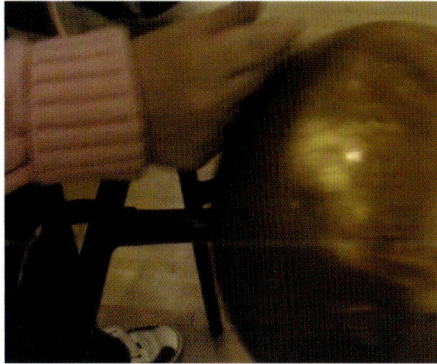

"SHE IS GOOD AT BOWLING." (CLAIRE'S FRIEND)

"SHE GOES OUT. WE GO FOR NICE WALKS." (CLAIRE'S FRIEND)

Young person
Beteena Apps

Artist
Annis Joslin

"ACTION!"

BETEENA WAS ANXIOUS ABOUT LEAVING SCHOOL.
"I WANNA STAY WITH MY FRIENDS."

"(I LIKE) LOOKING AT ART WITH MY MUMMY."

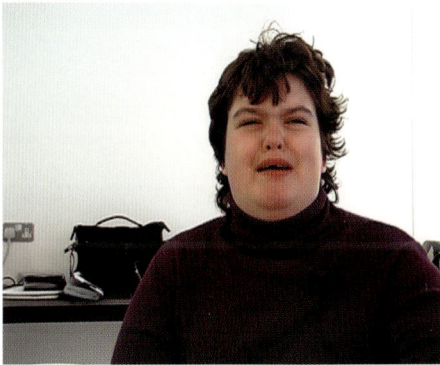

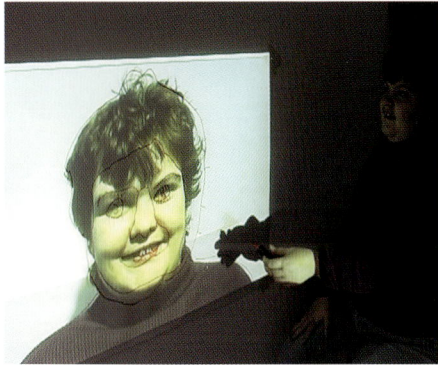

Young person
Loren Jerome

Artist
Annis Joslin

LOREN LIKES BEING OUTSIDE AND GOING FOR WALKS WITH WORZEL.

"WHEN ARE YOU GOING TO PRESS THE BUTTON?"

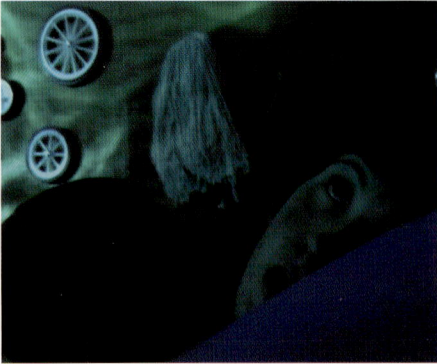

ON THE TRAMPOLINE.

"LOREN JEROME."

Young person
Husne Tekagac

Artist
**Tim Corrigan and
Charlotte Ginsborg**

"SHE'S SO CLEVER. YOU CAN TELL FROM HER FACE. WHEN THERE'S SOMETHING BAD, SHE GETS UPSET BUT WHEN THERE'S SOMETHING GOOD, SHE SMILES AND LAUGHS." (HUSNE'S SISTER)

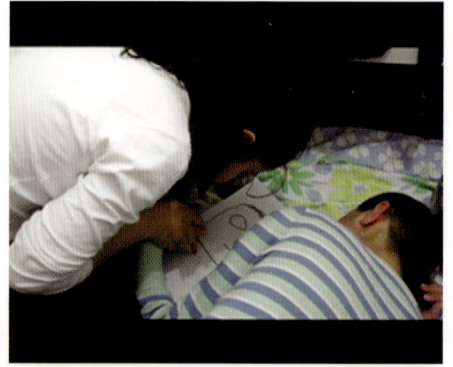

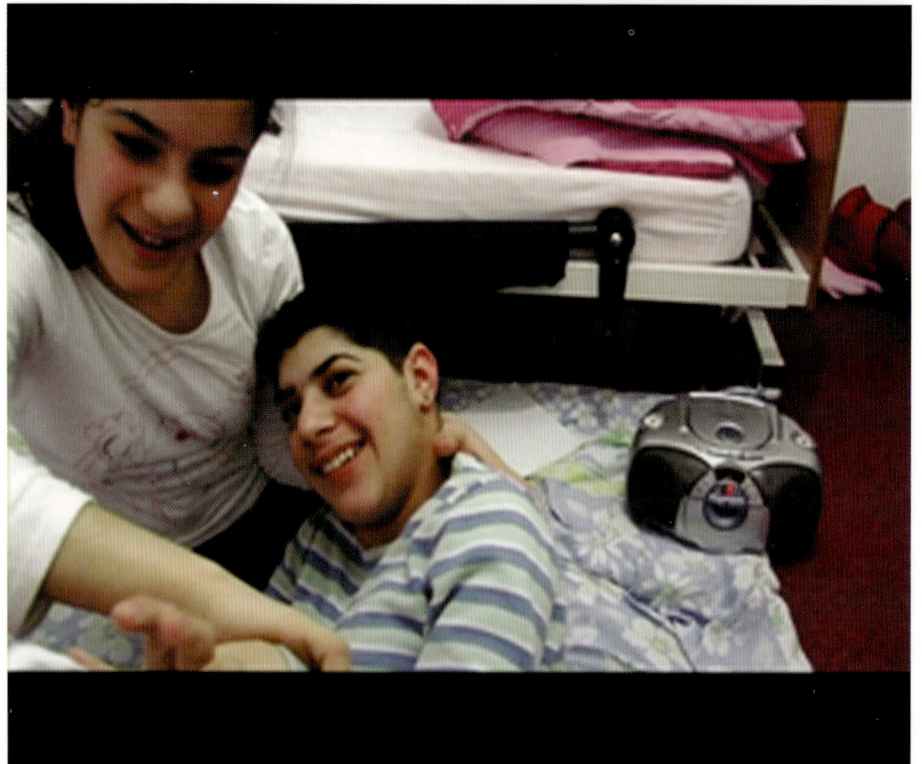

"WHEN SHE WANTS TO LISTEN TO MUSIC, SHE SIGNALS
TO ME AND TAPS THE RADIO." (HUSNE'S MOTHER)

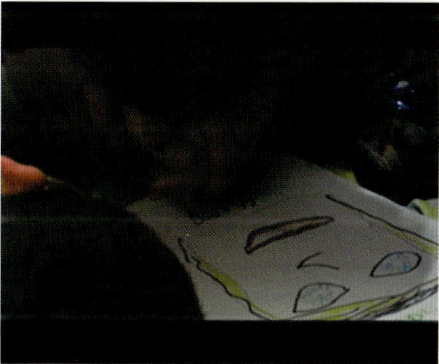

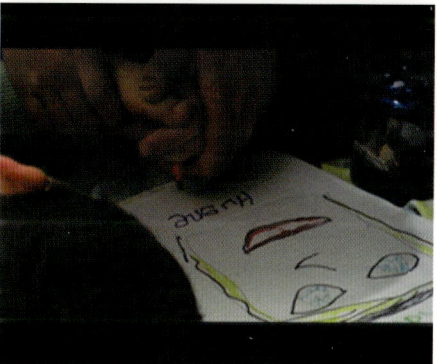

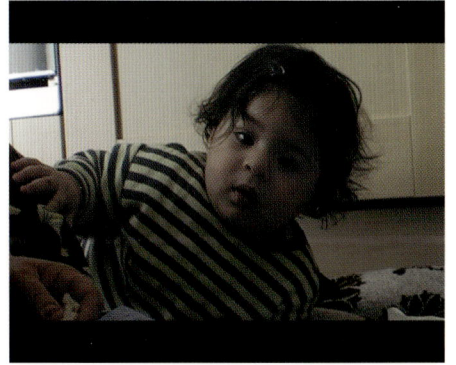

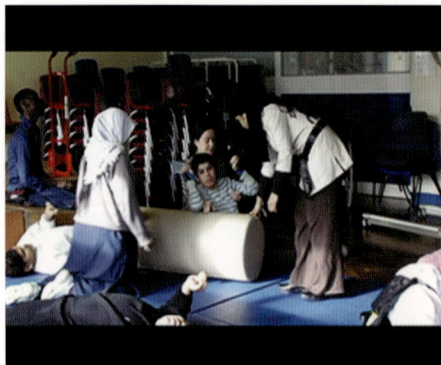

"SHE LIKES GOING OUT WHEN IT'S SUNNY. SHE LIKES LISTENING TO MUSIC AND WATCHING TV AND PLAYING THE GAMES THAT SHE LIKES. IF THERE IS A PERSON THAT SHE SPECIALLY LIKES, SHE LIKES TO MEET THEM." (HUSNE'S SISTER)

67   Husne Tekagac | Tim Corrigan and Charlotte Ginsborg

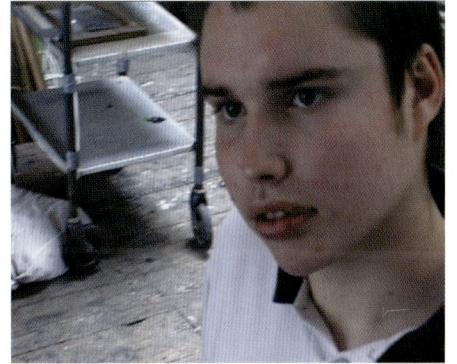

"JON. I WANT SOME MORE PAINT."

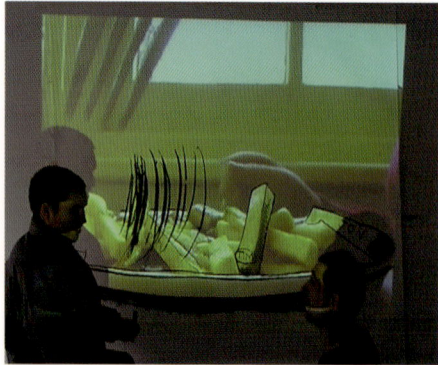

"I WANT SOME STONES. I WANT ANOTHER ONE."

"I WENT TO SCHOOL. I'VE BEEN ON THE COMPUTER. I DONE POSTMAN PAT."

Young person
Sophie Bristow

Artist
Shona Illingworth

"FOR SOMEONE WHO CAN'T SPEAK, SOPHIE'S INCREDIBLY VOCAL. YOU KNOW SHE'S THERE." (SOPHIE'S MOTHER)

"AS SHE'S MATURED SHE'S ALSO GAINED INDEPENDENT SKILLS.
I THINK SHE IS MORE HER OWN PERSON." (SOPHIE'S MOTHER)

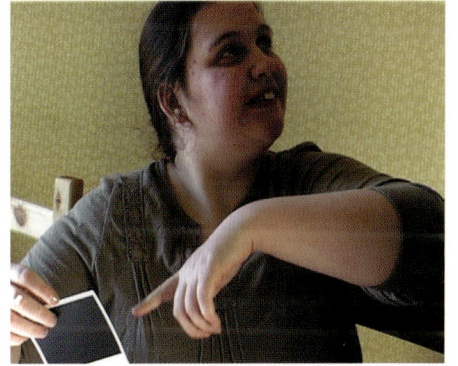

SHE GIVES VERY GOOD FOOT MASSAGES.

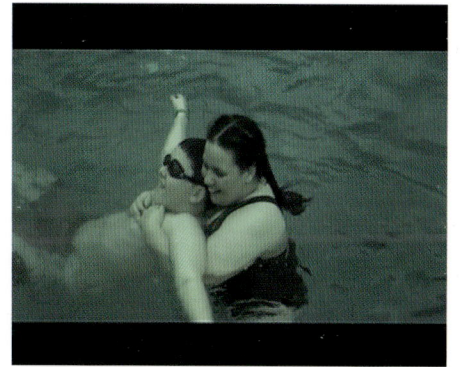

SOPHIE HAS GREAT CONFIDENCE IN THE WATER.

Young person
Jack Stephenson

Artist
Ben Rivers

"HE'S ALMOST OBLIVIOUS TO WHAT IS GOING ON AROUND HIM. HE SEEMS TO HAVE A VERY SIMPLE AND REWARDING LIFE." (JACK'S BROTHER)

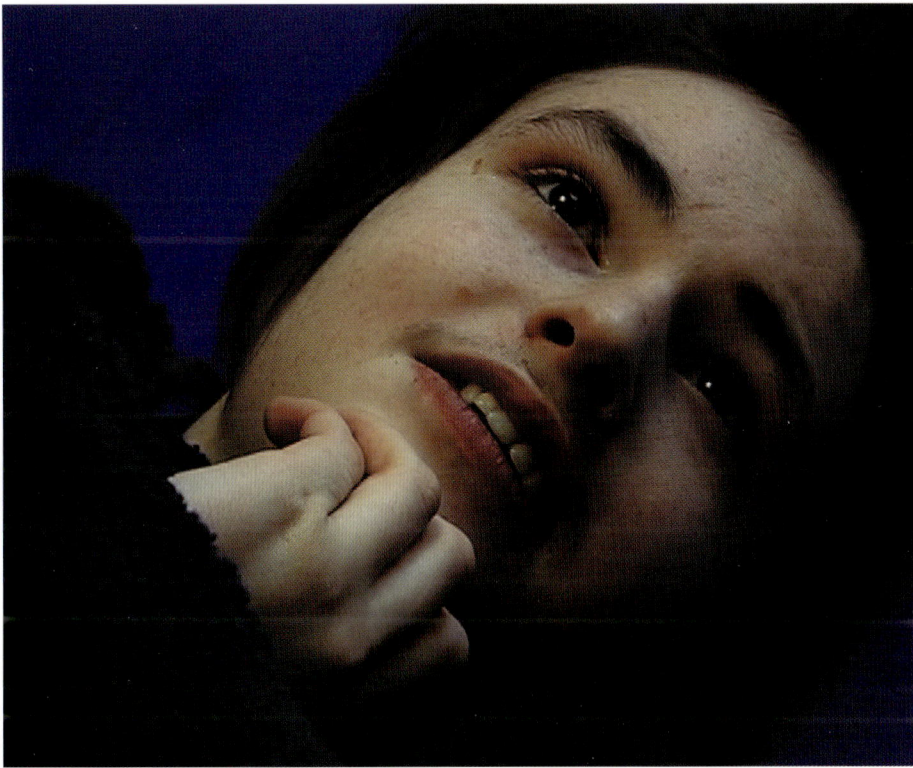

"HE NEEDS TO HAVE SOMEBODY WITH HIM ALL OF THE TIME, FOR HIS OWN
SAFETY, EVEN WITHIN THE ENVIRONMENT OF THE COLLEGE."(JACK'S TEACHER)

"THE ONLY COMMUNICATION IS TO TOUCH YOUR LIPS WHEN HE WANTS YOU TO SAY SOMETHING. IF HE TOUCHES THEN WE SING." (JACK'S BROTHER)

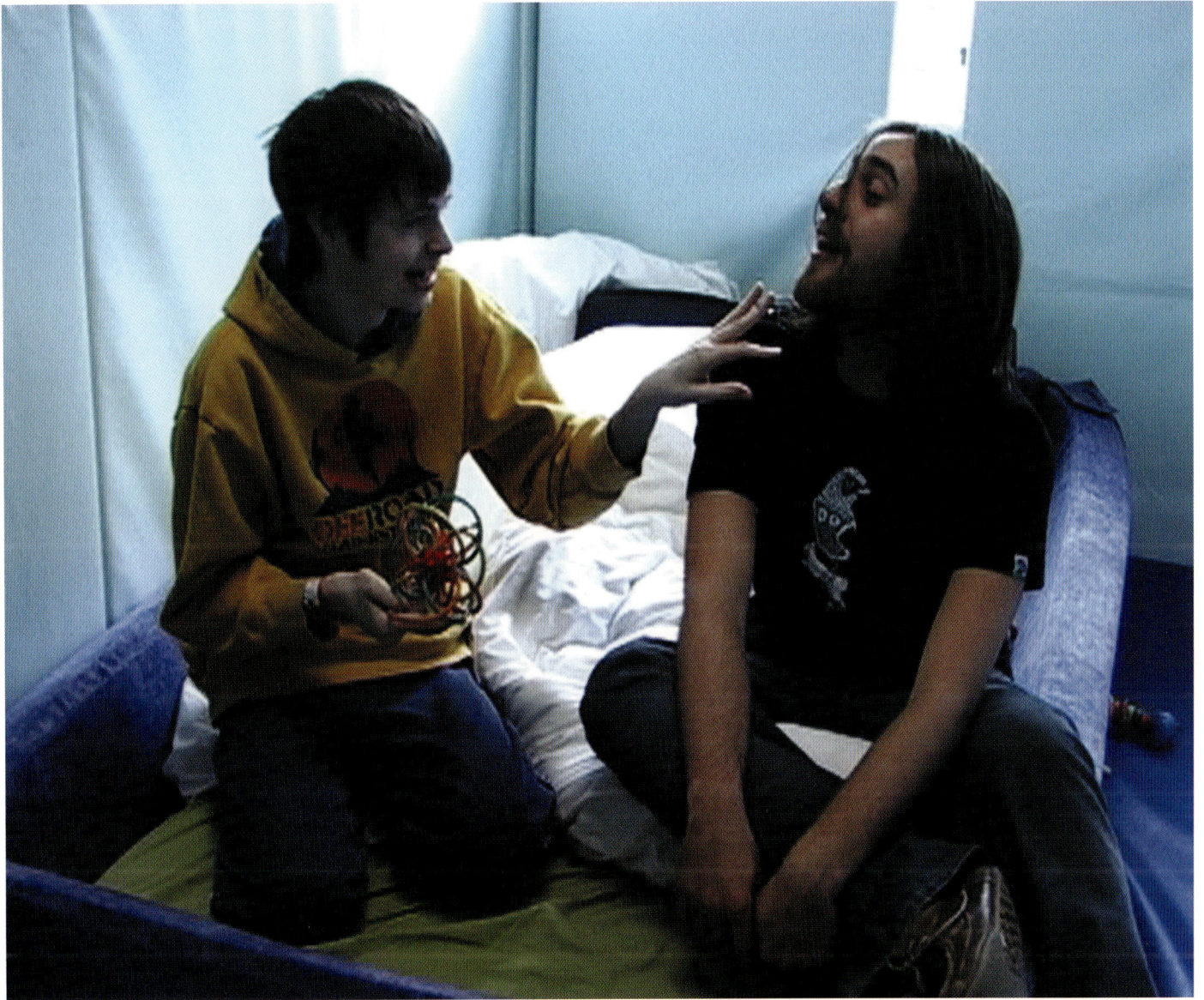

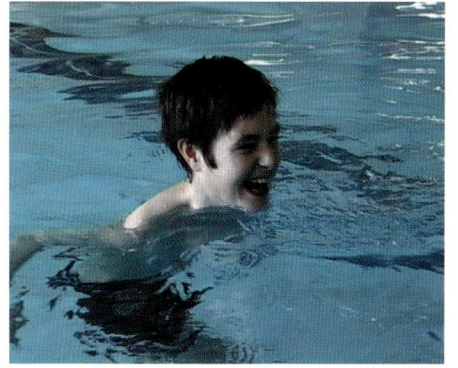

Young person
Helen Snowden

Artist
Annis Joslin

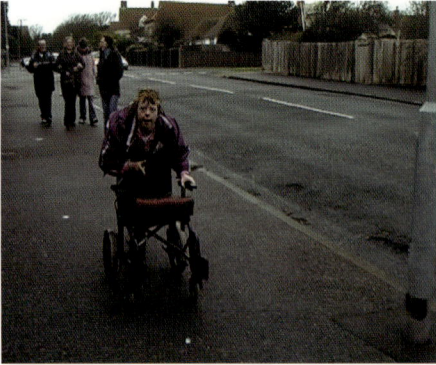

HELEN LOVES GOING OUT. SHE LOVES NURSERY RHYME
VIDEOS, FAIRGROUND RIDES, RIDING HER TRIKE, CUPS
AND SAUCERS AND PEOPLE BEING AROUND HER.

SHE LIKES BUS RIDES AND TRAIN RIDES
AND WATCHING BABIES AND TODDLERS.

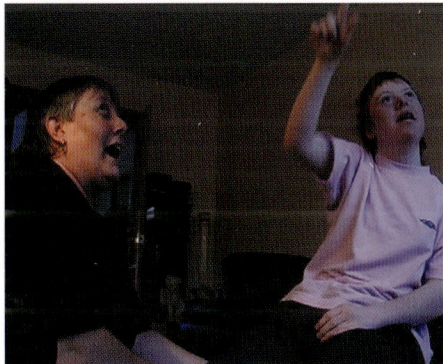

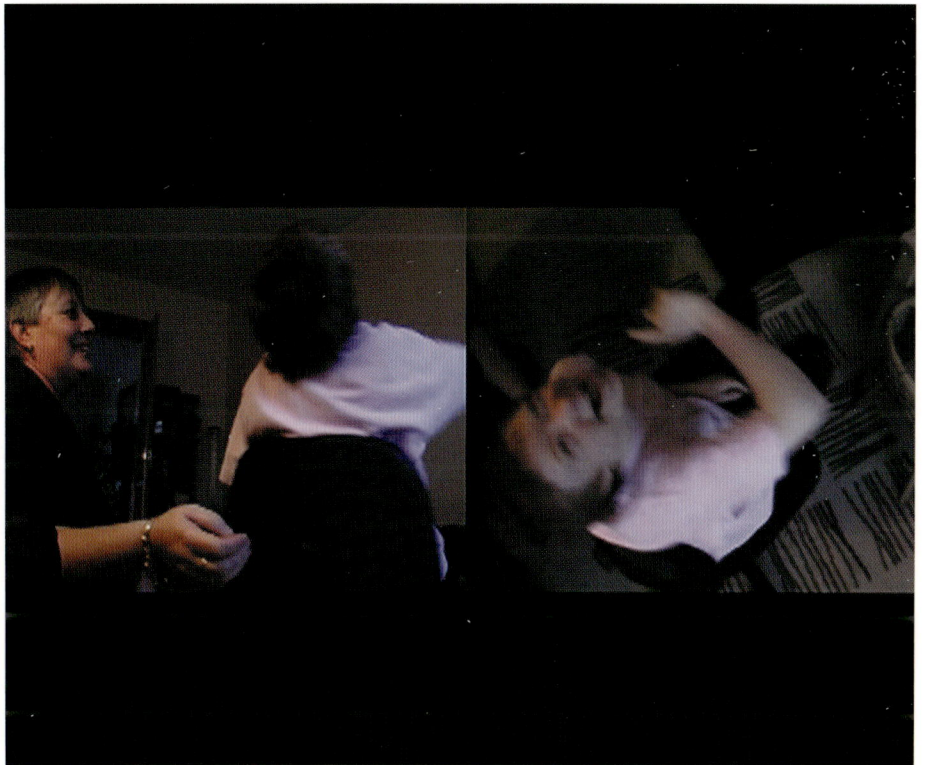

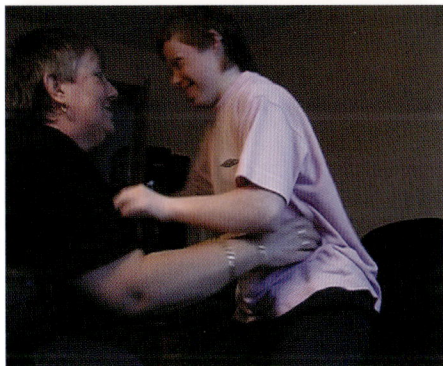

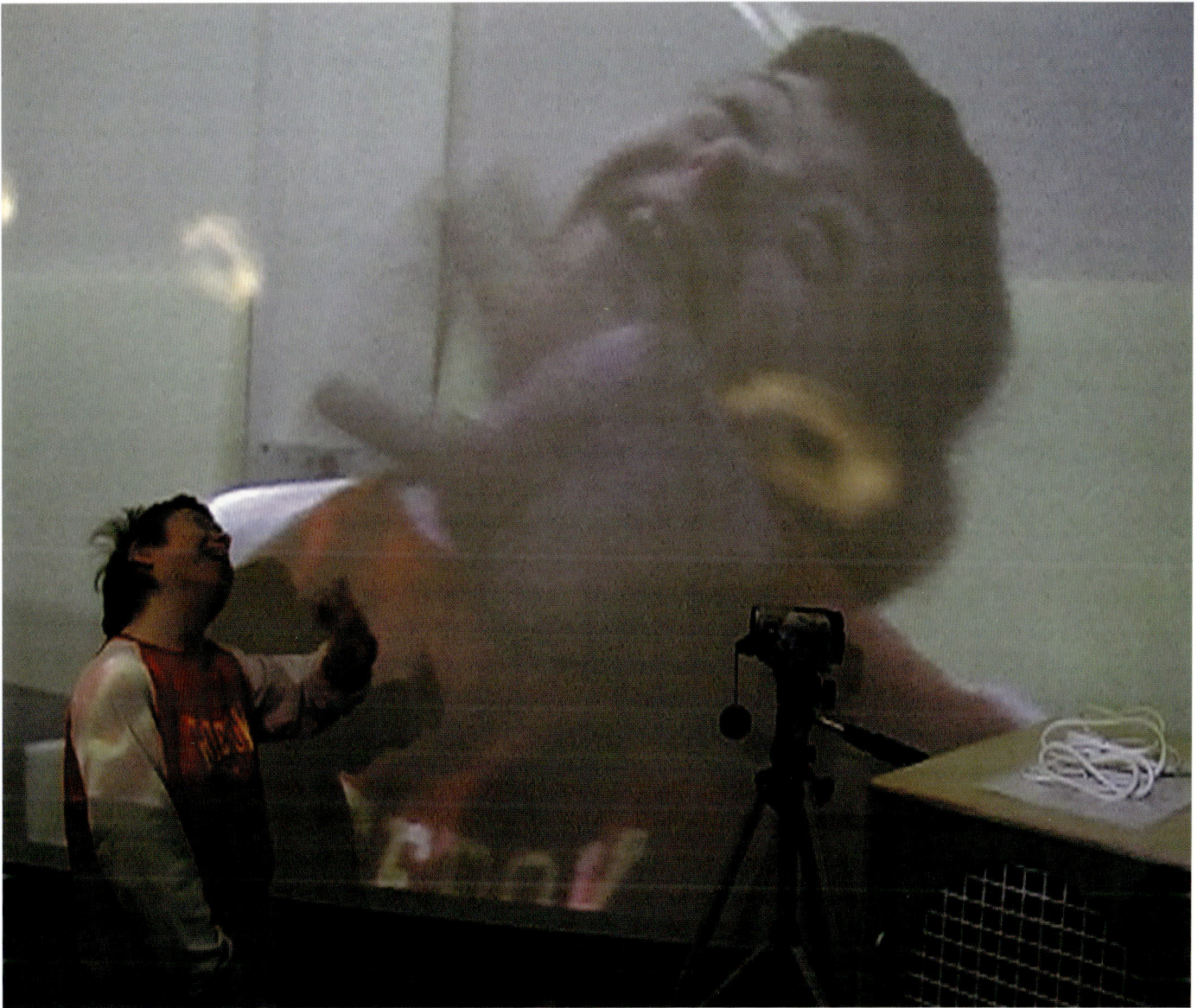

SHE DOESN'T LIKE ANY ANIMALS, OR WALKING TOO
FAR, OR SEEING CHILDREN BEING HURT. SHE DOESN'T
LIKE WEARING HATS, GLOVES OR SUNGLASSES.

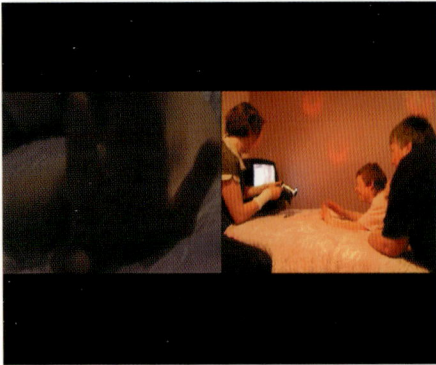

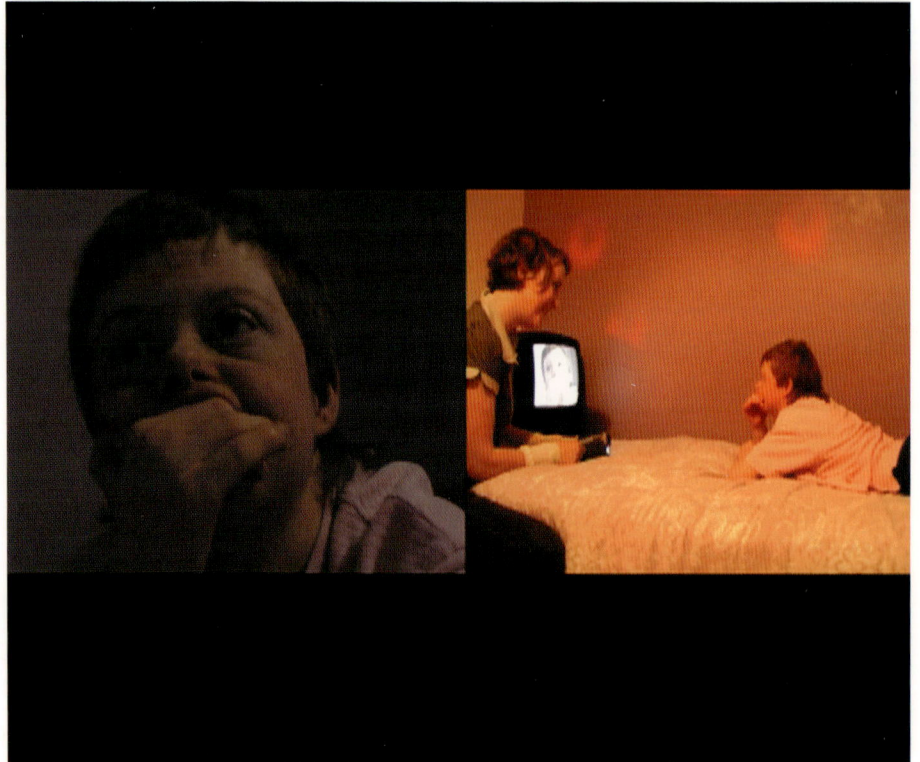

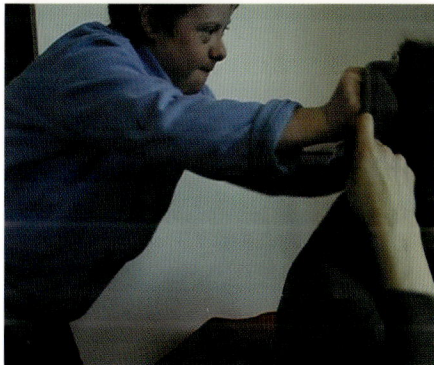

Young person
Hannah Cottingham

Artist
Shona Illingworth

"THIS IS MY ROOM. I WATCH TELLY IN HERE. I SLEEP IN HERE. IT'S ABOUT THE RIGHT SIZE FOR ME. I LOVE THE COLOUR."

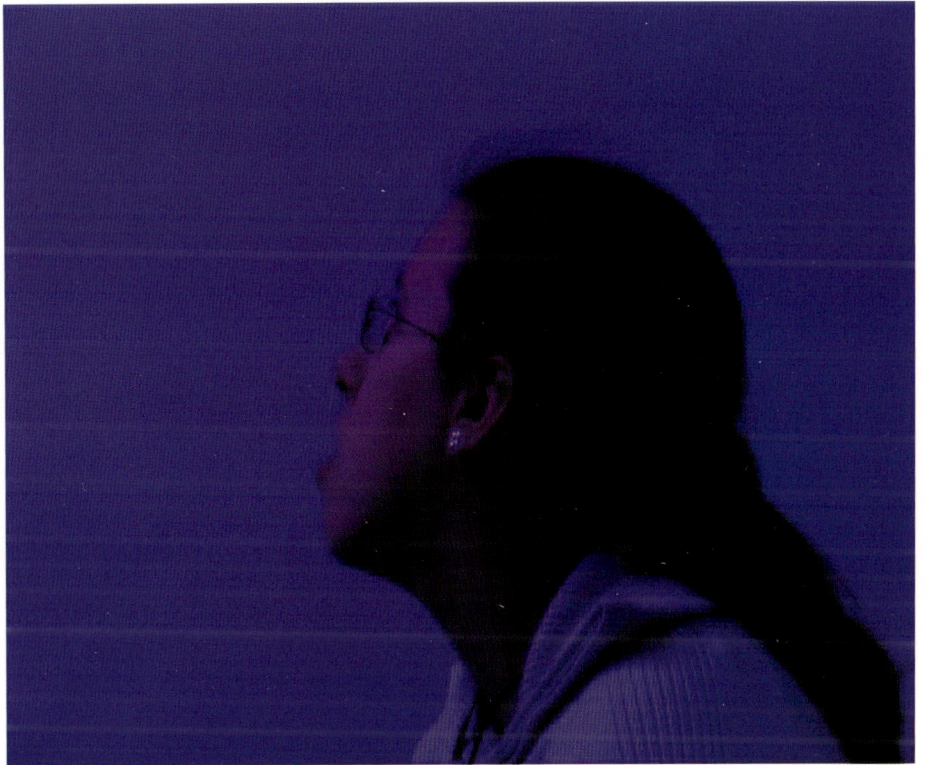
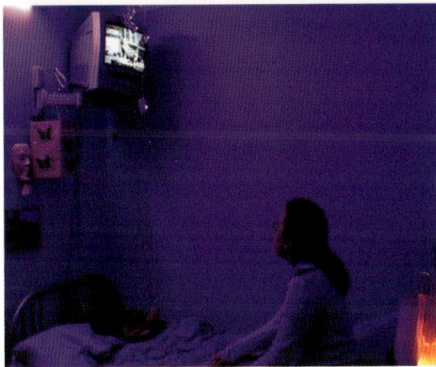

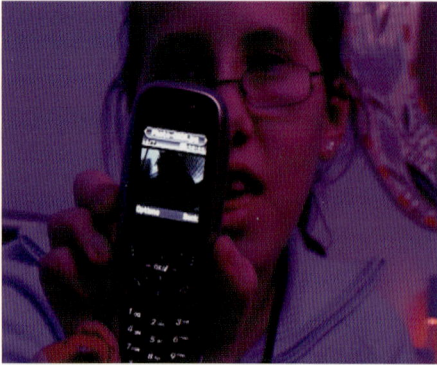

"I TEXT PEOPLE, PHONE PEOPLE AND TAKE PICTURES."

"LOVE IS YOU WANT TO BE
WITH SOMEBODY WHO
CARES ABOUT YOU."

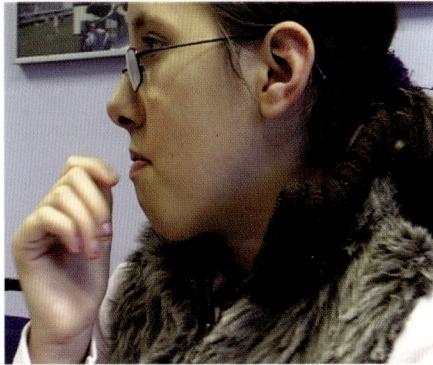

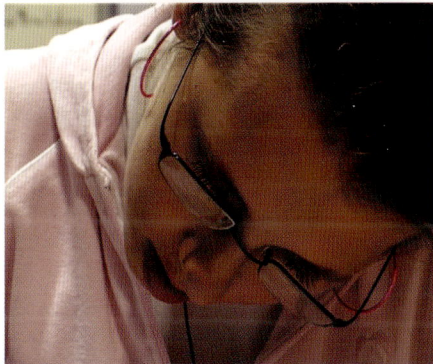

"DI SAYS I'M THE BEST P.A. SHE EVER HAD AND I SAY,
I AM THE ONLY P.A. YOU EVER HAD."

HANNAH IS A JEHOVAH'S WITNESS AND ENJOYS
GOING TO MEETINGS WITH HER FAMILY.

"I LIKE DOING HORSE RIDING. IT'S REALLY GOOD FUN. IT MAKES ME FEEL LIKE A PRINCESS. IT MAKES ME FEEL LIKE THE HIGHEST PERSON IN THE WORLD."

Hannah's Riding Lesson

Lessons learned

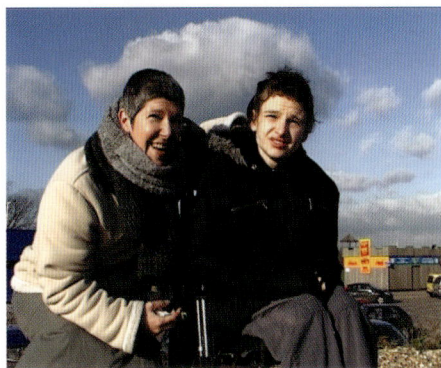

The Personal Profile Project was designed and delivered by artists. Its medium was the moving image. Six artists worked with 12 young people to make films that would help them 'to communicate something about how they perceive the world'. The young people communicated with the artist and through the artist. They communicated with people who knew them well and with people they had never met.

While the objective of each of the 12 collabarations was to produce a film that would make an impact on its target audience, the process itself made a significant impact on those involved in it. The films offered insights to professionals, support services, families and wider audiences about the creativity, life and potential of each young person.

The project aimed 'to give a better understanding of each young person, beyond their disability, by describing their preferences and individual qualities, in ways that were accessible and poetic'. An unexpected outcome was the extent to which people living with, teaching and working with the young people on a daily basis developed new perspectives and insights.

The project had unexpected results for family members who found themselves reflecting, on film, on their relationship with their child or sibling; who saw the young person behaving in different and sometimes unexpected ways in their absence; and who realised the significant contribution that the film could make to changing opinion, policy and practice in relation to young people with complex needs.

It is not uncommon for parents to express surprise when they see film of their child rising to a challenge, or experience it at first hand, for example in a school performance. Families' reactions to film footage of their child or sibling painting on the beach, or listening to music in a relaxation room, or joking with a care worker at a respite centre fall into this category.

The same kind of new knowledge was acquired by social workers and teachers when they saw footage of young people in their own homes, interacting with siblings and pets and walking in the countryside, far removed from the more familiar classroom setting or respite home.

The process of collaboration involved in making the films seemed to foster, in some cases, a greater sense of what was possible and a willingness to invest more resources in turning those possibilities into realities.

The timing of the project meant that not all the films could not be completed in time for them to be used by social workers to present to social care funding panels making decisions about specific individuals. They have, though, been used to introduce young people to new social workers and carers and parents have talked about being able to explain, with greater confidence, the person their child is.

Parents' awareness that, as a result of the films, the professionals who work with their children might gain a better understanding of their lives outside formal structures and institutions does seem likely to have increased families' sense that they are better understood.

Although the films were commissioned as individual pieces, the combined impact of 12 films, amounting to almost three hours of viewing, is considerable in artistic as well as educational terms. By producing films that are good to watch and easy to read, the project has helped to ensure that the young people recognise themselves in them, that families feel a sense of ownership of them, that they can be cited in evidence by social workers to their panels and that future care providers can use them to learn something about the young person with whom they will be working. In this way the project has achieved its aim of 'facilitating greater participation in the assessment and description of a young person through art'.

An installation, designed by Project Art Works, in which all 12 films can be seen simultaneously and this publication are now bringing the lessons learned from the project to a wider audience. Young people with even the most severe and profound disabilities are shown as having strong, vital qualities of individuality, humour and strength.

What next?

Project Art Works will facilitate and support artists of distinction to collaborate in the making of films with a further 36 young people in the South East. The artists and social care practitioners involved will continue to explore the impact of creativity, art and film on the processes of transition while seeking to utilise more fully and to extend the integrated methodologies and partnerships that are crucial to successful planning and support for young people as they head into adult life.

At a critical time of transition, these films and collaborations will engender a climate of possibilities around a young person and a greater investment in them by family, professionals and peers.

More information

Useful leads

Connexions
www.connexions-direct.com

Department of Health
www.dh.gov.uk

Foundation for People with Learning Disabilities
www.learningdisabilities.org.uk
Tel (enquiries): 020 7803 1100
Email: fpld@fpld.org.uk

Learning & Skills Council
www.lsc.gov.uk
Tel (help desk): 0870 900 6800
Email: info@lsc.gov.uk

National Autistic Society
www.autism.org.uk
393 City Road London EC1V 1NG
Tel: 020 7833 2299. Email: nas@nas.org.uk

Person-centred planning
www.helensandersonassociates.co.uk/Reading_Room/

Scope
www.scope.org.uk
6 Market Road, London N7 9PW
Tel: 020 7619 7100

Social Care Institute for Excellence
www.scie.org.uk
Goldings House, 2 Hay's Lane, London SE1 2HB
Tel: 020 7089 6840

Triangle
www.triangle-services.co.uk
Unit E1, The Knoll Business Centre,
Old Shoreham Road, Hove, East Sussex BN3 7GS
Tel: 01273 413141
Email: info@triangle-services.co.uk

Valuing People Support Teams
www.valuingpeople.gov.uk

Useful publications
Person-centred planning
Dowling, S, Manthorpe, J and Cowley, S (2006) *Person centred planning in social care. A scoping review* Joseph Rowntree Foundation
www.jrf.org.uk/bookshop/eBooks/9781859354803.pdf

Marchant, R, Lefevre, M, Jones, M, Luckock, B (2007) *Children's and Families Services Knowledge Review 18 'Necessary stuff': The social care needs of children with complex health care needs and their families.* Social Care Institute for Excellence
www.scie.org.uk/publications/knowledgereviews/kr18.pdf

Rettie, R (2003) 'Connectedness, Awareness and Social Presence'. Paper presented at the 6th International Presence Conference, Aalborg University. www.kingston.ac.uk/~ku03468/includes/docs/Connectedness,%20Awareness%20and%20Social%20Presence.pdf

Sanderson, H (2000) *Person Centred Planning: Key Features and Approaches*
Joseph Rowntree Foundation

Government documents

Department of Health (2007) *Modernising adult social care – What's Working*
www.dh.gov.uk/en/Publicationsandstatistics/Publications/

Department of Health White Paper (2001) *Valuing People: A New Strategy for Learning Disability for the 21st Century*
www.archive.official-documents.co.uk/document/cm50/5086/5086.htm

Department of Health (2007) *Valuing People Now: From progress to transformation*
www.dh.gov.uk/en/Consultations/LiveConsultations/DH_081014

Department for Children, Schools and Families (2007) *Aiming High for Disabled Children: Better Support for Families*
www.everychildmatters.gov.uk/resources-and-practice/IG00222/

Prime Minister's Strategy Unit (2005) *Improving the life Chances of Disabled People*
www.cabinetoffice.gov.uk/strategy/work_areas/disability/

Wider reading

Foucault, M (2003) *The Birth of the Clinic: an Archaeology of Medical Perception.* Routledge Classics

Bachelard, G (1969) *The Poetics of Space.* The classic look at how we experience intimate places. Beacon Press

Golan, O, Golan, Y, Baron-Cohen, S, Hill, J (2006) 'The "Reading the Mind in Films" Task: Complex emotion recognition in adults with and without autistic spectrum condition'. Social Neuroscience, Volume 1, Issue 2, pp 111-123

Zeki, S (2001) 'Essays on Science and Society: Artistic Creativity and the Brain'
Science 6 July 2001: Vol. 293. no. 5527, pp. 51 - 52 www.sciencemag.org/cgi/content/full/293/5527/51

Epstein, R (2002) 'Consciousness, art and the brain: Lessons from Marcel Proust'
http://ccn.upenn.edu/epstein_web/epstein_proust_prepub.pdf

Levine, J (1983) 'Materialism and Qualia: The Explanatory Gap'
www.umass.edu/philosophy/PDF/Levine/Gap.pdf

Lodge, D (2002) *Consciousness and the Novel.* Secker and Warburg

Sinason, V (1992) *Mental Handicap and the Human Condition: New Approaches from the Tavistock.* Free Association Books

Re Transition Profile Pilot with Project ArtWorks

My daughter Cherry and I were invited to participate in this amazing Pilot Project over three years ago. At that time we were trying to plan for Cherry's transition from the familiar routine of school and children's services, to her unknown future as an adult. Our biggest worry was how we were going to introduce her to a whole new world of people who didn't know her as well as we did.

To be clear, Cherry does not talk or express herself with any kind of direct language. To know what she is thinking or feeling requires 'tuning in' to her, very personal, range of communication techniques. It also requires you to 'assume' that there is someone who is listening and has stuff to communicate, even when direct 'replies' may not be forthcoming. Understanding Cherry takes a little time and a lot of trust. Project ArtWorks had been working with her for several years and had seen in her the talented, expressive young woman that she was becoming. We agreed to participate immediately.

The process of filming was enjoyable. It helped us to focus our thinking around who Cherry was capable of being and seeing her through the new eyes of the artist/film maker really made us look harder at our own assumptions about her. Once the film was complete we began to show it to all the people who were trying to get to know Cherry to help her develop her new life. These were people who were making assessments and writing reports; people who were planning for care packages and choosing what services would be appropriate to offer her.

It included people who would be providing personal care for her and people who would be commissioning services for her future needs. Without exception they found this form of introduction to Cherry to be the most helpful in getting to know about her quickly. Seeing her on film, in her life; being happy, sad, cheeky, sleepy and grumpy; interacting with her environment and the people in it, they immediately accepted that she had a real awareness of herself and others. The questions on their assessment forms didn't capture that.

Now Cherry doesn't have to 'prove' herself. The film makes her very clear to all. Since that first year, when we met so many new friends who benefited from the insights in the film, I have shown it to student social workers doing their BA or MA Degrees at Sussex University as part of my work bringing real experiences into the classroom. They are all amazed at how well they understand Cherry from just ten minutes. Again and again this little film proves itself and allows people to revise their assumptions about 'hard to reach' individuals.

The making of this profile was also instrumental in helping us decide to set up a web site for Cherry so up-to-date pictures and information could be made available about Cherry and her family and friends for new people in her life to see. Now I don't have to introduce Cherry to everyone. She can do it for herself.

Angela Lane

© Project Art Works
Arch 3, Braybrooke Terrace,
Hastings TN34 1TD
Telephone: 01424 423555
Email: info@projectartworks.org
www.projectartworks.org

ISBN 0-9541014-3-X

Collaborators: Beteena Apps, Liam Ash,
Sophie Bristow, Hannah Cottingham,
Claire Day, Mark Fraser, Loren Jerome,
Cherry Lane, Anisa Mayet, Helen Snowden,
Husne Tekagac, Jack Stephenson

Artists/Filmmakers: Tim Corrigan,
Charlotte Ginsborg, Shona Illingworth,
Annis Joslin, Andrew Kötting, Ben Rivers

Project Coordinator: Jo Giles

Funders: The Camelot Foundation
Arts Council England, South East
East Sussex County Council

Writers: Kate Adams and Phyllida Shaw
Designer: Dean Pavitt @ LOUP
Printers: Graphicom, Italy

Project Art Works would like to
acknowledge the creative contribution
of Jon Cole to this project.

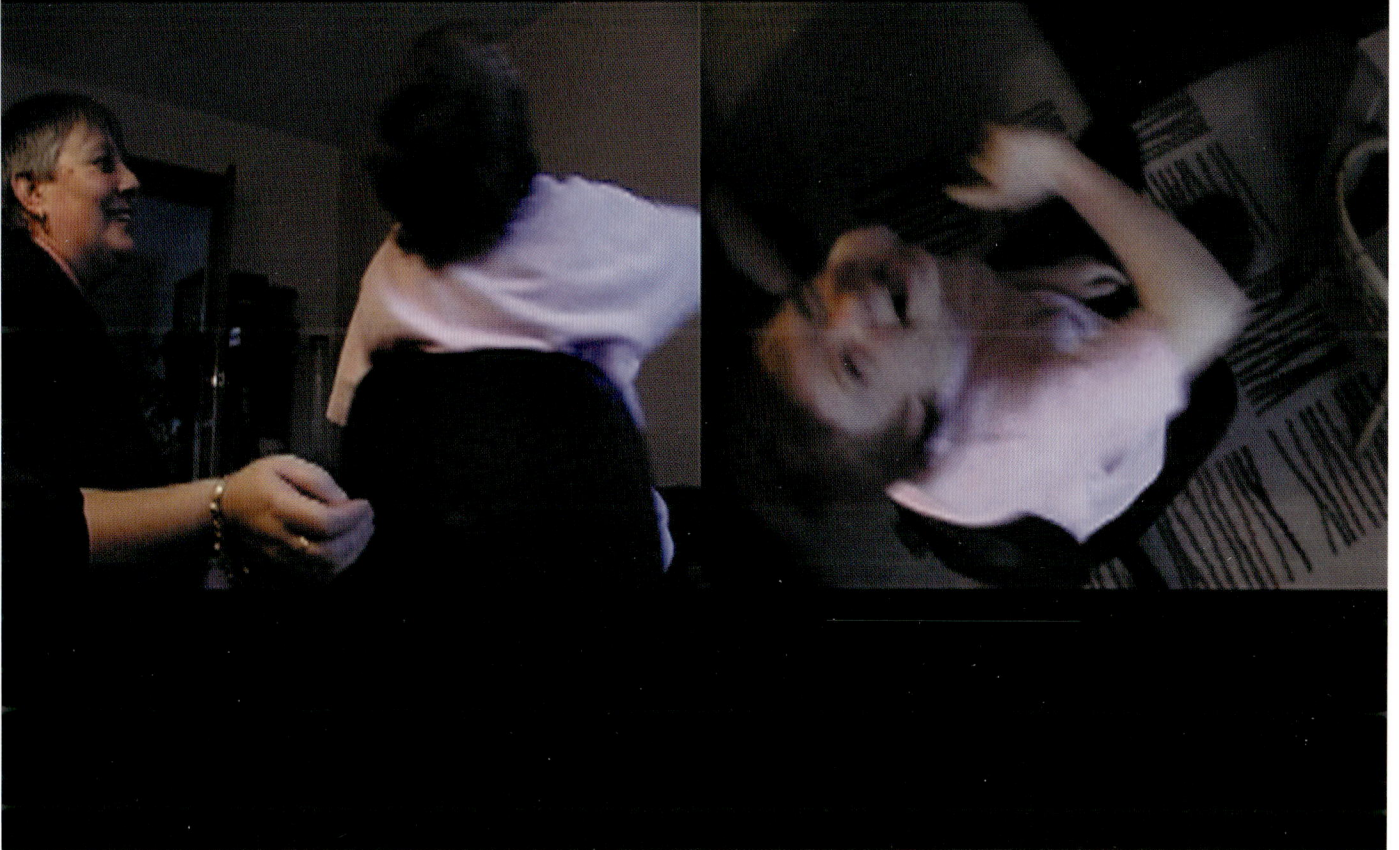

The design of the project

The origins of the project